How to Write, Edit, and Self-Publish Your First eBook

Make Money Writing Instant International Bestsellers!

By Gerry Marrs

ISBN-13: 978-1499300857
ISBN-10: 1499300859

DEDICATION

I'd like to thank my two kids, Gary M. and Ashley who are a complete joy everyday to be around and have fun with. Thanks for accompanying me on this life journey; I know it hasn't been easy.

Table of Contents

Introduction

Be prepared to embark on a life changing experience, one that's finally puts you in the driver's seat of your life. Too often, we become the slaves of our jobs, our material possessions, creditors, and basically anyone else that holds out their hand expecting us to share our hard-earned resources. What if I told you that you can have all of it and still have enough to share? Imagine being able to take the vacation of your dreams and have an automatic machine making money for you, all while you are enjoying precious time with your family.

Using this automated way of making money is by no means a small feat. You must be dedicated and willing to make a few small sacrifices to make this work. That, and be open minded about seeking the advice of others to become the ultimate information producing expert yourself.

In the 80's, information marketing involved a number of different subjects sold via catalog or ads placed in magazines. This method involved targeted marketing, and was most certainly a numbers game and small numbers at that (where the ratio of readers to responses was actually less than 1%).

The 90's was considered the Dawn of the Internet, as households began to commonly access information streams, but among those sources of information, money-making opportunities seem to invade the consciousness. If you were looking for ways to make money, the information was out there or at least for a small fee. Some of this information was useful and some, complete garbage, but at the time, the only people truly making money were those selling and marketing the information and not so much the readers.

Today brings a new opportunity for people to share their ideas, knowledge, and imagination. Additionally, it's possible to turn these ideas into a steady stream of income using the latest technology as well as a wide market audience. The Amazon Kindle makes information marketing possible for anyone to make money, and their program is also flexible enough to allow marketers to set their own prices and even market our books for us without complicated classified ads.

This book will provide you with a path to get started on your road to information marketing using the Amazon Kindle eBook reader. I'm going to essentially lay out a road map that if followed, can put you on a profitable approach for your new information marketing calling and hopefully turn you into one of the many success stories.

They say new Kindle millionaires are being made every day. Imagine writing that book that rakes in six figures in the course of only a few months. Years ago it took finding a publisher and sifting through dozens of rejection notices. Now, you can skip ALL of the middle-men and become your own publisher, your own editor, and most importantly of all, your own boss.

So be prepared to absorb this book, highlight information where needed and get ready for a new exciting chapter in your own life.

Gerry Marrs
gerry.marrs@gmail.com

Chapter 1 - Why Write?

This may seem an easy question to answer for some, as writing may come as a natural ability; however, for the rest of us, squeezing our thoughts on paper might be a labor intensive as doing chores or painting a house. It must be done, but works out a lot better for everyone if it's enjoyable. Perhaps you are the type to hold in a ton of ideas but have some difficulty putting those thoughts on paper. It's difficult to look at the big picture of writing a book and consider how many words and time one must dedicate towards making a book reality without being really discouraged or quitting before you begin.

Manageable Sized Projects

The best way to tackle any project is to chop it down into bite size pieces. For writing a book, those pieces might often be in the form of chapters or even down to lines. A roadmap in the form of an outline can define the shape of your book, and once you have everything in place, the words seem to flow automatically and some authors even claim that the book begins to write itself after awhile.

In these next several chapters, I will provide some ideas to help guide you through this process. You may or may not even have a solid idea in place yet, and if that's the case, I hope you find this book useful enough to stimulate your own creative impulse and maybe even become inspired to create your own eBook.

Success Stories

Let's take a look at a few success stories to give you a few ideas how lucrative eBook self publishing can be.

Amanda Hocking was employed as a group home worker up until 2010. During her free time she wrote 17 novels which she subsequently self-published. One year later, her sales were well over a million copies downloaded, earning over two million dollars in sales. She now regularly achieves 9,000 downloads per day.

You do the math. At 9,000 downloads per day with at least a $2 profit is $18,000 per day, or $72,000 per month!

John Locke started as an insurance salesman who became the first author to sell over one million eBooks through Amazon. He is now a best-selling author and now teaches others his success at selling 1 million books in five months using the Kindle system. Imagine reaching only a quarter of that with even only $1 profit per book. That could pay off your house!

A search of the Internet can provide you with a trove of other real-life examples. The question you should be asking yourself is, are you willing to put forth the effort and time involved in writing a book? How can you get in on the information market? What ideas do you think people would be most interested in hearing from you? I carry a small notebook with me wherever I go, and as new ideas occur to me, I write them down whether they make sense or not. Later you can go back, look at your notes and see if anything sticks.

Finding Your Personal Niche

While I'm currently working on my first fictional novel, the nonfiction market has captivated my interest for years. I was a self-professed opportunity junkie in the early nineties and as such, read every book I could get my hands on regarding mail order, information selling, and home business opportunities. The ground truth is, the only people making real money from this information were the ones writing and creating the opportunities. "How to" booklets could be found in full page ads in most popular magazines (which cost thousands to advertise so someone had to be making money to pay for this). My favorite title used was, "How to Legally Rob Banks," which really enticed my interest and was a very successful marketing catch-phrase for years. Someone used the power of their imagination to create something and also made a ton of money doing it too.

Stimulate Your Imagination

So, I recommend that you do something to kick start your imagination. Taking a long walk somewhere picturesque can clear your head and allow you to start free associative thinking; just let the ideas flow. No, don't try to skip ahead a few chapters to check out the mechanics of this system, you really do need some proper motivation to get this started right. Maybe start off with imagining yourself getting paid, and gradually replacing the income from your job. Perhaps you just want to take your family on a vacation somewhere nice (like Florida), or even just to upgrade your car. You need to find that something that stimulates enough passion inside you to get you moving. For me, it's the thought of being a full-time writer and moving away from the 9 to 5 grind. What really moves me is bringing my kids to Orlando, Florida (pick any theme park you like). To extend that experience and not have to go back to work would be a dream come true. So, my brain begins to work overtime on the creation process even while I'm there.

Ask Many Questions

I find myself asking questions internally, such as, what do I already know? What topics do I have the most experience on? What topics would be most read by the public? I realize that the latter question requires some market research, but during this self-reflective analysis it's not necessary to know this just yet. The idea is to get your creative thinking processes moving in a forward direction. As you come up with ideas it would be a good idea to jot down some notes. Don't be formal with your notes, just write. If you need to draw a picture, that's okay too, some people work better using symbols as shorthand.

Imagine being able to make money from something you've created from your brain. It requires no resources other than your natural intellect, talent, and experiences. Whether you take the nonfiction approach or invent new characters you bring to life in e-print, all it takes is a little motivation to make things happen.

Once you've found your spark, the next step is just as critically important.

Set Writing Goals

Goals are like tasks, broken down into reasonable steps that can be accomplished in realistic timeframes. Popular literature on entrepreneurial success suggests that when one writes down their goals, along with a reachable date, they are 90% more likely to hit their target than those who don't write them down.

Writing your goals down should meet some basic guidelines;

1. Goals should be specific and well understood (not vague)
2. Goals should be measurable (Certain markers should be identified to know once a target has been reached)
3. Goals should be reachable (if the goal can never be reached then it may encourage burn-out)
4. Goals should be realistic (based on your available time for instance, you might only be able to crank out 1,000 words a day, that's okay)
5. Goals should be timely (lengthy goals may result in loss of interest)

You should post this list where you can review it every day, but not where it becomes part of the background scenery. Two most commonly favored places are either the kitchen refrigerator or the bathroom mirror. You should look at your list at least once a day, usually in the morning when you're planning your day. It helps if you can post it publically, where psychologically you will hold yourself accountable in adhering to the list.

It certainly helps to check off items as they are completed. This will give you a sense of closure before tackling the next goal, whether it is a page, chapter or whole project, attainability is what will solidify your power of belief.

Realistic writing timelines might include daily word limits or weekly number of pages. Most authors use the word counts in popular word processing software to track word counts and don't stop until their daily limit is reached.

Free Software for Writers

There are free software programs available that will help you track your writing goals, perform word processing functions and even organize your thoughts as you write. One such program that I highly recommend is called yWriter by Spacejock Software:

(http://www.spacejock.com/yWriter5.html).

The software is nearly an all-in-one word processor and scene-to-chapter development tool. It is perfect for breaking up your project into bite-size workable pieces. Also, this program was designed by a novelist so you know you're getting a professional package by someone who has been there, like you.

I've reviewed several other novel-writing programs but none of them provide the functionality of organizing your work like yWriter. Breaking your novel or non-fiction piece into scenes, allows you to set small goals and actually set a completion timeline. Additionally, if you like yWriter please register the software with the creator.

Chapter 2 - How to Capture Ideas

Well, after you've seriously considered taking on this project, now it's time to come up with a topic. Preferably, a subject that stimulates all your passion and interests and perhaps just enough to motivate you every day to keep writing. One consideration is whether you will pursue fiction or a non-fiction genre for your first eBook. Some new authors never consider the preparation work involved in the latter, since non-fiction will require an extensive amount of research to present credible, factual information, if one wishes to develop any type of fan-base. There will be a sizable amount of time involved, unless it's a subject you are well experienced enough to expand upon. Fiction will require imagination, and as long as you follow plot-lines in some comprehensible fashion, you can well enough manage your writing time without distraction. Some research will be involved in fiction writing too, but relies more on what's already inside your head. Credibility is still important, even to a good fiction writer, so be sure to research your topic thoroughly or someone will certainly point out your errors in a future review.

Blogs and Surfing

So let's discuss how to generate new ideas. Assuming you have internet access or at least a way of surfing the web, many new authors like to review the latest market trends online. One such way is to review blogs on the latest books being self-published. I found a really great blog written by Bob Spear (http://bobspear.wordpress.com/) that takes a look at such current trends along with some valuable demographic information. It's possible your work may involve targeting a particular audience and if that's the case, this website would be a good starting point.

Search engines such as Google, provide an immense source of links. Using the keywords, "reviewing market trends to write a book" yields some 71,800,000 results; however, while this seems an absurd amount, you'll most likely find what you need in the first two or three pages.

Experiences

The best source of ideas may come from your own experiences or even those of a family member, neighbor, or friend. A story doesn't just happen in one sitting either; it can be something that starts off as a simple idea and then other experiences build upon that. The story begins to expand and then you have a basic plot in which to develop an outline, and so on. Sometimes the best ideas come from long walks or an event where you can isolate yourself from all things such as ambient noise, traffic, television, and yes, even loved ones.

Combination Thinking

Some authors have been known to combine two or three stories into one. Take for instance the story from Star Trek: The Wrath of Khan, which combined some elements from Moby Dick. The theme of relentless pursuit combined with space adventure created a story all its own. It's not uncommon to recycle really great plot lines and make them all your own. Many successful authors do this and some strongly view it as following a proven success formula. The key is to make the story your own, add in your own elements, and create a spectacular ending to bring it home.

Tools

An important tool in your arsenal of creative thinking should be a notebook and a good pen or pencil. Much of what I'm about to tell you may be linked to your own personal preference; however, you need a place to jot down ideas as they happen. The notebook you buy should not be pretty nor have elegant designs on them as many will have a tendency to not want to write in them. You can jot down expanded notes or small symbols as a memory jogger for later. Two people can see two completely different things when watching an event, and the same holds true for conceptualizing ideas. One method may work differently for another, such as one author might prefer outlining a whole storyline rather than piecemeal bits of ideas. Some authors I know like to storyboard, drawing actual mini-scenes before they even pen a word. A popular motivational writer keeps a notebook by his bed, scribing ideas the moment he wakes up. Some believe that this is the premium time to write ideas, since the logic side of your brain has not fully activated yet, which would ordinarily inhibit the best creative ideas.

Collecting and Gathering

Another method of building up ideas is gathering interesting articles as you read, clip them, store them (in a box) and over time you will have enough conjugated ideas to develop a story. Certainly the notebook will help you form a storyline from this box. Some authors I know will randomly pull articles from the box, place them side by side, and imagine a story. Think of this as the A-B-C method, "always be collecting" which will be discussed more in depth in the next chapter.

As you sit in a quiet place or perhaps somewhere on a long walk, you make come up with a fantastic idea; however, you should not get caught up in the details at this point.

Top down/bottom up

Another great method is to use a "top-down" or "bottom-up method.

 An example of using a top-down method would be to think about the big picture and work on the details later. For instance, you can say that your story is about a lawyer that was offered a great deal of money to lose a case. Now you can refine and think about questions like: what case, how much money, why lose it etc. Those questions will lead you further, and will probably help come up with new ideas and plot elements.

A case of using a bottom-up approach would be to develop very fine detail from the start, and build it from the ground up. For example, Mr. Steven Jones, a lawyer, finds an anonymous letter on his desk with the words "drop it" and a photo of his wife and children. Now, you can think about his reaction. Does he call the police? You can envision talking with his secretary and ask her who came into his office during his absence? In detailing his actions, you can then come up with more ideas, until the entire plot comes to fruition.

Brain-Storm or Spider-Chart

I like to brainstorm ideas on paper, though there are lots of pieces of software available – these might be useful if you want to develop an idea into a full article, as they allow you to move things around.

For the low-tech method, though, just grab a bit of paper – a full blank sheet of computer paper works well, as it's good to give yourself plenty of room! Write your topic (maybe the name of your blog, or the subject for a short story writing competition) in the center … and start jotting ideas around the edge.

Timed Ideas

Set a stop-watch for five minutes and start writing. Write down as many ideas as you can within that time, and don't stop. The objective is to keep your pen moving, or keep typing away, until the timer stops.

The pressure of time can force you to be creative and you will find yourself writing things down in almost frantic desperation to beat the clock. When you look back over the ideas that you've developed, you might find that some phenomenal ideas have appeared.

Lists of 50 or 100 Ideas

In addition to the stop-watch method, you can also create a numbered list that defines a more orderly way of organizing random ideas. In your notebook or a word processing document, number a list from 1 through 50 (or 100). Start writing down ideas as they occur. It may even seem random at first but after awhile you may see a pattern develop. This is your subconscious mind in action.

Don't stop until you hit your number goal.

A sideline challenge would be to combine this with the stop-watch method and see where it takes you.

Joining the Dots

This involves drawing lines to connect related ideas together.

Usually, one idea will not be sufficient enough for you to write a whole story or article from it; but several points could be better combined to form an overall plot. Alternatively, one topic may be far too general, so sub-points may be the key to recall or reinvent details later.

If you are developing ideas for fiction, combine ideas from opposite sides of your page; merging two different compositions can give you that initiative you need to come up with something truly creative.

Think of your brain as a muscle that must be exercised regularly to stay in shape. Many writers practice various exercises to stimulate their imagination and develop these new ideas with the use of writing prompts. You can use your favorite internet search engine to find the many free tool available worldwide. Some of these prompts with provide you with a key phrase "Describe a perfect world..." and leaves you to quickly fill in the rest. Combine this with other methods and you will have created a great starting point to launch your next novel. In the next chapter, we will discuss how to gather resources to research your new eBook idea.

Chapter 3 - Gathering Resources

Fiction or Non-fiction?

Before you begin to develop a good research strategy, you should be certain whether you are going to pursue writing fiction or non-fiction as a genre. While some may believe that the research processes are essentially the same, there are certain nuances that are important to remember as you build your information portfolio. For instance, when writing a non-fiction book, you will want to present sound, credible information so your customers will write a good Amazon review. In this case you would want to become quite the expert on whatever topic you are writing about, whereas a fictional story may take less convincing. The term "artistic license", lets you fill in those informational gaps, and does not put your credibility at risk as much as non-fiction writing can.

Time

In chapter 4, we will discuss timelines for the actual writing of your book; however, you should also consider and set aside time for research as well. You might choose to combine your research and writing, which is a perfectly acceptable scenario; however, some authors like to compartmentalize tasks such as building up their knowledge first and then developing ideas from this collection of material.

Best time to research

You might be a morning person, a lunchtime taskmaster, or even a "before-bed-project" kind of writer. Either way, you'll want to find the right time to dedicate to your research each day. This can even be combined with writing if you multitask during the day. For instance, you might spend your mornings looking up information and writing your story or article in the evening. You can certainly finish your writing faster if you follow this two-segment approach.

Time management

Time management is something the majority of people don't think about unless they have to juggle multiple routines. Perhaps you have small children or family activities to manage. Unless you set the time aside to work on your book, your agenda will be competing with higher prioritized events in your life, thus subject to random moments whenever you can find the unplanned time to do research.

Setting timelines and goals

So what kind of timelines and goals should you set to get started? It really depends on how much expertise you don't already have. In other words, if you're writing about a subject you know absolutely nothing about, the timelines will be longer than a subject in which you are intimately familiar with. You'll want to set specific target dates such as, "I want to complete my research 3 weeks from today and the completion date is November 4th." The important thing to do is write this on a calendar and set it as a solid goal.

Money

Money is a rarely talked about issue when it comes to writing and creating eBooks. To some, writing may be a free sport or a hobby that one uses as artistic expression, but, this eBook is written to show you how to make money too. The old adage, "it takes money to make money" is still true, even when it comes to writing and publishing in the eBook market.

Basic necessity

As a necessity, money provides you the all basic needs of life such as food, water, shelter; but, it can also be used as a tool to help you leverage more by increasing the chance of more buyers through investing in your own work and by making your eBook more attractive to readers.

Use money to improve your book

We tend to hold much bias when it comes to our hard earned time spent creating our eBook. Not only do we overlook critical details, such as spelling and grammar; but even omitted words altogether as our brain records what we think we've written rather than what's actually on paper. This is where paying for someone to review our work may be the key to improving your writing and getting your eBook ready to sell.

Hire editors

One way is to hire someone to review and edit your eBook. The price for this kind of service can be rather expensive though, but the end result may be the different between a successful publication versus receiving bad reviews for inappropriate grammar and bad spelling. Additionally, this could seriously jeopardize your credibility. Putting away some money for future editing may be a smart idea if you want to become a serious author.

Hire writers

Some eBook sellers subcontract out their writing if they are not confident at their own skills or perhaps someone they know has a better idea that they are willing to market for them. The focus of this eBook is to create your own material but there are writers out there available for a fee if you find time lacking for writing your own material and are willing to pay for someone to do this. Some writers have no issue with being paid and having someone else take the credit as publisher. One excellent source is iWriter.com. You can also make money writing small articles as well as hiring other authors to help you complete your projects.

Hire cover designers

Unless you are a graphic artist, you'll probably want to hire someone who has that kind of talent. The price for this kind of service can range from a measly $5 up to a professionally crafted illustrated cover for $1,199 (from CreateSpace, an Amazon sponsored company).

As a goal

Of course the reason you probably bought this book is to make money through something you created. They say that the more you invest, the more you can potentially earn; but, with the right talent, I say you really don't need to spend a great deal of money to publish your eBook. Many independent authors started with nothing but a hope and a dream only to achieve wealth through repeat sales, great reviews, and a huge following. If this is what you want, then you've come to the right place.

Information

Based on your genre selection (non-fiction topic or fictional story), you should have developed a list of what areas you need to focus on for your research. Your "brainstorming" notebook is still the best place to jot down this list and it will keep everything in one convenient place when forming your outline.

What are you looking for?

Any type of research normally starts at a broad level and then can be broken down into sub-topics that paint a bigger picture. For instance, you might be researching a topic about dieting. One might start with the broad topic first, such as the overall dieting effect on the human body, and then work down to different types of diets and how fast they work or don't work.

Types of information

Something very important to keep in mind while collecting information is that there are different types of informational sources you should be aware of.

Librarians and scholars label these as primary, secondary, or tertiary sources. It's important to remember that some of these sources may be considered more credible over others.

The best research source is primary data which is considered "firsthand" obtained information.

Primary information is comprised of original materials that were created first hand. This type of information is from the time period involved and has not been filtered through interpretation.

Some great examples are diaries, interviews, letters, original documents, patents, photographs, proceedings of meetings, conferences and symposia, survey research and works of literature.

Secondary information is found from material that is considered second hand data. This source is made up of accounts written after the fact with the benefit of hindsight. It is comprised of interpretations and evaluations of primary information. Secondary information is not evidence, but more like commentary on and the discussion of evidence. Some great examples are biographies, books, commentaries, dissertations, indexes, abstracts, bibliographies (which are used to locate primary & secondary sources), and journal articles.

Tertiary sources are thought of as third hand knowledge.

Tertiary information is a concentration of primary and secondary information. A few examples of this are almanacs, encyclopedias, and fact books.

Sources

So now that you understand the different types of informational sources, you'll need to know where to look to access them. There are a ton of free sources available to anyone and yet some will require a fee or some form of subscription service. This eBook will focus on saving you the most money and accessing free information where available.

Internet

Of course this is the largest source of information, some it credible and some highly suspect. For being a free source of information though, it remains unbeatable. Once you master how to do a search, you can find just about anything online.

Search engines

When searching for information, rather than use a question, type in a phrase instead. For example, if you ask the question, "What is the best method to use for planting tomatoes?" you should use the phrase "tomato planting instructions." Narrowing down your search from a broad phrase is helpful too if you want to avoid too many search results (such as, "tomato planting instructions in a Greenhouse").

References

Wikipedia is one of the Internet's most recognized information database, encyclopedia, and reference tool all in one! As a matter of fact, the Amazon Kindle uses Wikipedia when allowing users to lookup highlighted keywords. Wikipedia is a collaboration of edited, multilingual, and free Internet encyclopedia articles supported by the non-profit Wikimedia Foundation. Wikipedia's 30 million articles in 287 languages, including over 4.3 million in the English Wikipedia, are written and edited collaboratively by volunteers around the world.

Library

One would think with today's Internet that libraries would be obsolete, but this is not the case. Libraries have access to a vast array of historical books, documents, and most anything in print. The best part is it's free to join! Other reasons might include having access to a librarian, someone who is specially trained in doing research and can advise you where to look.

Most libraries now have access to an electronic database of their books which makes finding what you need so much easier. Also, you can find books that are no longer in print but hold valuable historical information whether your writing is about history, politics, or even business.

Free access to databases is another perk of using your library system. These databases store valuable articles about a wide range of topics, most of which can't be found in an ordinary magazine. These are articles publishes in professional journals such as business and psychology and in some cases these are accepted by the scientific community as proven fact since they go through a very rigorous testing process prior to being published.

As you can see, the library is still very much a viable and relevant tool for active researchers.

Chapter 4 – the Act of Writing, Outlining, and Timing

So now you've got a story to tell or a nonfiction subject that you know will sell and make you make some cash.

The best way to do this, obviously, is to write it!

When you are a bookworm and read on a regular basis, you may think that writing is as easy as reading. Besides, writing a book just entails you to put together ideas in an organized manner that would make sense, right?

Wrong!

Writing a book is so much more than that. It involves a lot of work, sleepless nights, criticism and many more. And to think that this is just the beginning! But, of course, we're here to help you out! Here's a quick guideline on how you can make the writing process of your book a lot more uncomplicated that it seems.

Develop an Outline

Making an outline works. Ask any author, writer or journalist out there. The very idea behind making an outline is so that you can organize your ideas, thoughts or plot. Take this outline as an example:

Introduction

Create Chapters

Chapter 1: Title of Chapter 1

Chapter 2: Title of Chapter 2

Sub Chapters

And so on and so forth.

Basically, it allows you to make a summary of the ideas in the draft. This way, you can easily encode where you want to place your thoughts. It would also help to place a small description of what you want to achieve per chapter. Believe me when I say that making an outline can slash your writing time by 50%. You would be surprised at how efficiently an outline can help you.

If you've tried writing a draft in the past and found yourself mixing up ideas and not making sense, this is the solution. Remember, readers want to read a book that flows very well from start to finish.

Structure

A lot of newbie authors believe that structure just happens, that it naturally sets itself as soon as you start writing. A structure, on the contrary, actually takes a lot of time to decide on. It is part and parcel of creating an outline.

Structuring a Fictional Book

For a fiction novel, you will need to start with identifying the elements involved in the story. This includes the following:

- Main and Supporting Characters

- Setting - Time and Place of story

- Problem – the main conflict in the story

- Solution – how the conflict is solved

- Establishing a point of view – 1st, 2nd or 3rd person

- Theme – what message are you trying to get your readers to understand?

After these elements have been established, it's time to create a structure like this:

- Beginning – how does the story begin?

- Climax – the very core of the story where readers will have trouble in putting down the book.

- End – how will the story end?

It is up to you as the author to decide on how to introduce the characters of the story, the conflict and other elements. You will want to create different rise and falls of climax. This way, there will be many exciting pages in your book, not just in the center of the story. Some authors put a dangling end on the story for readers to buy the next part of the series.

Structuring a Nonfiction Book

For a non-fiction book, you will need text features. Simply put, text features are the elements of a non-fiction book. They are real and you must publish them with utmost credibility. You need to be sure of all the data you place in there and you need to do a lot of extensive research. The following are the text features that are found in a non-fiction book:

- Captions – descriptions for every photograph or image you will feature

- Glossary – definition of words that the average reader may not know

- Graphics – charts or graphs as an explanation to some points in the book

- Index – list of all the ideas featured in the book in alphabetical order.

- Subtitles – definition of headings

- Many more such as maps, table of contents, images and the like.

There are many ways on how to structure a non-fiction book:

- Time Sequence – Timeline of events

- Description or List – this is basically the listing of facts

- Cause and Effect – describing something that happened and then describing its effects

- Compare and Contrast - comparing how facts are the same or different

- Problem and Solution – introducing a problem and educating a reader on how it can be solved.

- Material

How much detail do you want to put into your book? I'm sure you've seen an Anatomy book that is so thick and explains every function of every vein, cell and organ in the body in the same way that you have encountered a book that is entitled Anatomy for Dummies which is basically a crash course of the subject matter.

What is your goal for writing this book? Do you want to go into detail or to you want it to be short and sweet? How much material do you want to be in your book? This is something you have to decide on before writing because you have to be consistent with the material you provide. You can't have too much information in the first chapter and then present your reader with information overload on the next one. It just does not read well.

Length of Your Book

Different books have different lengths. The industry standard is 250 words per page for a book. And though they may not be a definite number of words or pages as a rule, here is a short guideline you could follow.

Length of a Novel

Novels – We are looking at 320 pages or 80,000 words. If you go below that, your book may be deemed as too short and if you go over 100,000, it may be deemed as too long. 80,000 words give the reader enough. If you have more ideas, just put it into a sequel. Besides, having more than 100,000 words means you will need to spend more for publishing. Take for example JK Rowling. The first Harry Potter book was relatively short. The subsequent novels were much longer because when the stories gained so much popularity; publishers basically just let Rowling write without setting limits!

Length of a Young Adult Novel

Young Adult – for YA's, 220 pages or 55,000 words is enough simply because these are light novels. Considering your target reader, you have to focus on a very interesting plot that is consistently interesting so the young adult continues to read it.

eBooks – When it comes to eBooks, you could go from the YA number to the Novel number depending on the book you want to write. Writers of eBooks still strongly recommend that short book lengths are what drive the most sales, so you do not have to spend an eternity writing an eBook if your goal is to make money.

Length of a Nonfiction Book

Nonfiction books should be clear, concise, and straight to the point. Many successful eBook authors starting out in the Nonfiction genre find success from 20 pages all the way through 100 pages; however between 30 and 50 seem the norm when you are first starting out. Don't stop at one book. Once you've completed and published a nonfiction book you should immediately start another one to spread your sales across different subjects until your first book becomes profitable.

Timeline

Is this different from the outline? Yes, it is. The timeline includes the outline, writing each chapter, editing, creating a cover, publishing and many more. It involves the whole process and it is important to make one because following a schedule will make it easier for you. For example, dedicate the first week of your writing process to making an outline. The next 3 months would be for creating the first draft. The next 2 weeks would be to edit. The next week would be dedicated to creating another draft and so on and so forth. When you create a timeline, the last part should show the target date for publishing. This will make you work faster as you are trying to reach a goal date or deadline.

Copying the Ideas of Others

It is just normal for writers to do their research and take inspiration from other author's ideas. But how far can you go? There is a very thin line between inspiration and plagiarism. Never copy what another artist said verbatim. If you shall use their ideas, make sure to pay respect and give them some recognition by citing them appropriately most especially in non-fiction books. You can, however, improve on another author's idea as we discussed in chapter 2. Perhaps you like a story and would have liked to have seen a different ending. Then rebranding an old idea may be the way to go.

Chapter 5 – Editing, Grammar, and Outsourcing

Congratulations, you have now finished the first draft of your eBook. But don't be tempted to publish it just yet! Every established author out there goes to a tedious process of editing before he decides to get his book out there. You should, too!

Why editing your eBook is important

Editing takes so much time and effort but must never be skipped. Here are the reasons why:

- Fictional Issues – If your eBook is fiction, you should not only be concerned with grammar and spelling issues. When you proof read your fiction eBook you might come across come inconsistencies with your characters that you need to correct. Don't worry, coming across inconsistencies does not make you a bad author. This just really happens with fiction drafts.

- Non Fictional Issues – When you've created a non-fictional eBook, you will need editing to double check facts. One simple error in the spelling of a source, term or date will automatically hurt your credibility as an author.

- Grammar Check – we simply can't leave this out of the list. Every ready is a grammar Nazi one way or the other! If they read something grammatically incorrect in your book, they will immediately think of you as incompetent.

Editing Properly

Contrary to popular belief, editing is so much more than just proofreading. It includes checking facts, ensuring the grammar is correct, and that the plot is consistent the story line. As mentioned above, it is a lot of work!

So here are a few tips you can use to edit your book on your own;

Tip # 1: Print Your eBook – traditional reading from a piece of paper is one tool that makes editing very effective for authors. They are able to place notes on areas appropriately in places where editing is needed and they are able to place bookmarks as well. Though this may be available in eReaders, nothing still beats the traditional post it note and highlighter method.

Tip # 2: Make A List of The Changes You Want to Make – once you have finished reading the eBook through, check out all the bookmarks you have made and create a list of the changes you want to make. For example:

- Make title more appealing

- Edit Chapter 1

- Change the name of main characters

- Cut some of chapter 10 and leave the final section

Tip # 3: Be Resourceful – when it comes to grammar and spelling, there are still a lot of arguments. For example, there is US English and then UK English. So you are going to decide on which one you want to use for your eBook. There are also different kinds of tenses that you need to be consistent with when editing. Though you can be sure that your English is of top quality, you will have some dilemmas along the way. If this happens, check Google Scholar and search for English rules and other related content to help you out. Google Scholar is a great source of legit and useful knowledge when it comes to editing. It will lead you to other websites that provide such services as well.

Tip # 4: Retype your entire EBook – Yes, you read that correctly – retype it! Don't simply edit from the original draft because you might miss something. So to make sure that you don't, just go ahead and start from scratch and use the printed output with bookmarks and notes as your guideline.

After all this, proofread it once more. Editing is a very challenging task but is worth every minute!

Battling Author Bias

Of course the book is amazing! You wrote it, right? Don't be too confident at this point just yet. You may have what we call author bias.

You are in love with your book because you worked very hard on it.

Remember, you are not the only audience once the book is published so it's best you ask for help from other people. Be prepared to hear some opinions you might not agree with, but make sure to stay professional and accept them as constructive criticism – so you create and publish a quality and unbiased product.

Here is a list of people or communities that you can turn to aid in editing your book.

Family and Friends – this group will never fail you and they would be glad to give you honest reviews. They will bluntly tell you what you might have missed and they won't ask for anything in return, except maybe for a free copy once the book is published. However, no matter how important the opinion of friends and family are, you will still need professional opinions which bring us to our second group of people.

Authors, Writers and Editors – if you don't know any writer's club within your vicinity, then you can check forums online to ask for some honest and professional opinion. Getting help from this people are valuable because they know what they are talking about and they can prove it to you. You might even come across some interesting debates from very educated people in these forums regarding grammar, writing style, etc. These forums are very interesting so it's best you register to one today.

List of Writers Support Websites

Here are a few sites that I've found are quite helpful to new authors:

Site	URL	Description
Absolute Write	www.Absolutewrite.com	Advice forum with a membership of over 30,000 writers
Critique Circle	www.Critiquecircle.com	An active online writing workshop with a multitude of free tools available
My Writer's	www.Mywriterscircle.com	Resources are

Circle		available for improving writing skills and a section to receive direct feedback on your writing.
Writing.com	www.Writing.com	Many free functions are available, contests, forums, writing circles, and a number of free tools.
National Novel Writing Month	www.Nanowrimo.org	You can join up with over 250,000 writers in writing a 50,000 word novel in 30 days. An online word counter helps you track your progress.

No Time to Do It Yourself? Hire Someone!

Are you living in a busy schedule and simply don't have time to edit it yourself?

Well, here is the solution to your problem – freelancers! Hire someone from the internet. Websites such as FIVErr, oDesk, Elance and the like feature thousands of freelancers who have experience in editing and can definitely edit your eBook.

Costs would depend on the freelancer's experiences and expertise. Of course, if you would be willing to pay a higher cost, then you are going to get a better finished product. Registering for these websites is free.

Start searching for the perfect editor and let him do a sample edit first before hiring so you can gauge his editing skills. Once everything is set, make sure to have constant communication with him so that you can update each other with the changes that need to be made. Once you are satisfied with the work, just go ahead and make the payment and keep his contact details just in case you need more editing in the future.

Editing requires serious skills in proofreading and knowledge in English grammar. It's not an easy job, but it's all worth it when you book sells!

Chapter 6 – Designing and Creating eBook Covers

They say that you shouldn't judge a book by its cover.

But let's be realistic here.

Every time a person walks into a book store and browses through bookshelves, they look at the cover of a book and they judge the contents by it. The cover of a book is very important.

It is the first thing you see and it will give you a reflection of what's inside!

In this chapter, we will discuss the importance of your cover designs and how you can make your own.

Why Does an Attractive Cover Sell?

Even if you believe that your book is the best out there, you won't gain traction with readers without an inviting and professional cover page. Established authors and self-publishing authors alike know this that is why they take a lot of time to create the perfect cover.

As mentioned above, the cover is the first thing that potential readers would see. If it does not blow them away, then they might not consider looking inside and therefore you would lose a sale.

Programs You Can Use to Design a Cover and Free Online Resources

There are many programs you can use to design a book cover. If you are a pro, then you can go for big shot applications such as Adobe. If you are not that experienced in graphics, Adobe may be a slightly more complicated for your needs. It is possible to create a simple AND professional cover.

Gimp

One of the easiest programs you can use is Gimp which is a free program for image manipulation that you can install in your computer that creates covers and other images. You can open a blank image, import and existing image and add the elements you want such as text or other clipart. Another program you can use is Inkscape which is like an easier version of Adobe and is also for free. But the best program you can use is Scribus which allows you to create the whole book layout including the cover.

Word

A surprisingly good cover design tool is to use Microsoft Word.

You can easily place graphics on a document measuring a normal 8 X 11.5 inch document and even add colorful text. There are a few good resources on the web that can help you design such a cover using Word. It is slightly tricky to save the file as a JPEG graphics files and you'll find yourself using two or three different software programs to get it right.

Format of a Cover Design

You have probably seen a lot of book covers out there and you have seen that there are so many kinds. There is no particular format to follow except the size but there are elements you need to include such as the following:

- Book Title – choose an intriguing title and make sure to place it in the cover

- Photo or Cover art – this can range from a photo related to the content, to the face of the author to a blank background. It all depends on what you want to place in there.

- Testimony – it would help if you place testimonies in the cover of your book. Quote a short caption from a reader who is popular and enjoyed your book.

- Your Name – of course, the author should be featured in the cover page. First and last name is required and credentials such as MD or PhD if there is any.

How to Make Your Own Book Cover

Here is a simple do-it-yourself guideline on how you can create your own.

Know that you will need two different files – the front cover and the back cover. So make sure to plan those out and not place too much information in front and nothing at the back. Usually title and author is in the front cover and summary and testimonials are on the back.

Decide on the binding of your book. There are so many book sizes out there and before you can start a draft on any program, it will need the dimensions of your book. It also pays to know how thick your book is so you can have the cover printed from front to back already. This way, binding would be an easier process and you get to save on expenses.

Decide on the art work you want to place on your book cover. As I have mentioned above, some people go as simple as a plain background or as complicated as top of the line graphics from established virtual artists. Well, it would be great to pattern the art work of your cover page from the theme or tone of your book. Take for example "The Fault in the Stars" by John Green. The book feels so melancholic and has a plain blue background in its front cover.

So what if you are not an artist? That's okay, because you are an author and you are not expected to know everything about graphics and art. You can turn to stock photography which is a supply of different photographs which are licensed that you can use for this purpose. But since they are licensed, you will to pay for them which is alright as well since it is still a lot cheaper than hiring a photographer or visual artist.

Stock Photography Resources

Here are a few websites that actually offer stock photography for a free download but will charge you for higher resolution files:

FreeFoto.com Plenty of images, organized in different galleries.

Dexhaus Good site with excellent photos

Kavewall A plethora of images and textures.

Digital Dreamers Different galleries.

StockVault Popular and good choice of photos

FreePhotosBank Another excellent cache of photos

FreeDigitalPhotos A treasure trove

Cepolina Many free images available in multiple formats

TurboPhoto Simple site and very to the point

FreeStockImages Beautiful website with awesome content.

DeviantArt Images, photo and Photoshop brushes.

DreamsTime   Hi-Resolution pictures are available

Unprofound A ton of images!

VintagePixel Old vintage style images.

OpenStockPhotography More than a million images are available

Drafting your cover

Create a few drafts of covers and ask the opinion of other people in order to see which fits your book the most. The best people to ask about this are those who have already read your manuscript. This way, they can tell if the cover page does justice for the content.

Hire Someone

If all else fails, you can hire someone to do it for you. There are thousands of freelancers in the World Wide Web who would create a book cover for money. Go to websites such as fiverr.com or odesk.com and create a client profile. After creating a profile, browse through the profiles of people by filtering artists, painters, virtual designers and the like. These are the people you want to hire.

When you create a job posting, place the important information such as what kind of task needs to be done and how much you are willing to pay for it. When people start applying, ask for their portfolio. You will want to view their past work so that you can see the quality of work they provide. If they ask for upfront payment, don't do it, because they might not finish the job. Check out their ratings as well. Ratings will show if they are a good contractor and if they have a good reputation as an artist. Usually, ratings go with comments as well.

Chapter 7 – Marketing

Your eBook is finally ready for publishing. And it's already a given that you are a great author. However, you may have some trouble selling your eBook if you lack experience in marketing tactics. Learning how to market can be very rewarding and actually quite fun. Here are a few simple suggestions for marking your eBook and getting the word out that you're published.

This is an easy crash course on marketing tactics that work magically with dispensing little to no cash at all.

Use the Power of Social Media

Social Media is used by millions, every day, in nearly every facet of life (news, sports, and family).

Facebook

For instance, Facebook has just hit the 1 billion user mark. Thus, using Facebook alone already provides you a market of 1 billion possible readers! Include Twitter, InstaGram and other Social Media websites as well.

You probably already have a Social Media account that you use for personal reasons. But using it for marketing your eBook is a totally different story. For example, let's discuss Twitter.

Twitter

Twitter allows you to engage with many other readers, authors and other people who are included in the target market of your readers. You can do casual conversation by reaching out through this people by tagging them in your posts regarding your new eBook. Once you have a lot of connections through twitter, you can take it up a notch by directing those people into your sites and e-mail subscription list. Once you get them there, you can offer the book and give them details about how they can purchase it and what it is all about.

Keywords

Most people who want to buy something go to the internet to search for it. The World Wide Web is a big mall for consumers where they can find just about anything they need. Your goal is to ensure that people who search for books similar to yours will land in your page and end up buying it. Your role is to ensure your page lands high in search engine results in order for more people to see it. Choosing the right keywords is going to boost your online presence.

Here are the things you need to keep in mind when using keywords:

- People key in short phrases in search engines. For example, instead of keying in "the best baking and cooking book or magazine", they would key in "best cook book" or "best baking book".

- Create a keyword list. Think of 3 to 5 phrases that your target market will key in when searching for an eBook. You can use Keyword Discovery or the Overture Keyword Tool in the internet to do this.

- Once you have chosen keywords, use them to create content on your blog and website. Feature these posts on your social media accounts so that your followers and other people in your network would be able to see it.

How Amazon Markets For You

You will become a great author someday and your books would be featured in many book stores all over the world. But for now, you must take advantage of the marketing programs of Amazon because it has one of the best online book databases in the planet at present.

If you have tried purchasing something from Amazon, you already probably know how it works. Here are the many ways on how Amazon helps you, not just in selling, but also in marketing.

- Once one copy is sold, your eBook is automatically ranked. It may not be ranked at the top, but it's a start.

- Get Amazon reviews. You can do this by asking buyers of your book to make a review for you. These are the star ratings you see whenever you browse through products.

- Browse through the top 100 best-seller list and see which topics are similar to your own eBook topic and then suggest it. This way,

you have a better chance at selling your eBook
to those who bought best-sellers as well.

- Make use of Amazon keyword tags so that
  searchers will get redirected to your listing.
  Examples of these keywords are "fiction" or
  "historical book".

- Join the Amazon Author Central. This is
  where you can have your own live author page
  via Amazon where you can feature a short bio
  and promote your other works as well. And,
  of course, a link to your eBook listing.
  https://authorcentral.amazon.com/

Using Amazon as a marketing tool may be a bit
challenging but it's the number one source for books
online and you can definitely benefit from it.

Get a Kirkus Review

Kirkus is an American magazine that publishes book reviews twice a month even before a book becomes available in the market (www.kirkusreviews.com). It was established 1933 and it is still actively reviewing books today. So you can be sure that when your book gets featured in Kirkus, it will be recognized by a lot of people and adds a great deal of credibility. This is something you can really rely on to get your book out there. However, it has a price and you will need to send them a copy of your manuscript – either a printed one or through PDF or Microsoft Word.

Another option is to create your book via CreateSpace.

CreateSpace

CreateSpace is a tool from Amazon which enables you to create your book in a more organized manner (www.createspace.com). It will review the interior of your book and aid you in creating a do it yourself cover for free. There are other professional services you can get hold of such as design, editing and marketing. There is a team of experienced professionals ready to offer you their services. It makes your eBook a lot more affordable and ensures you will get an ISBN. The other services of CreateSpace are paid but are totally worth it because you only need to publish and distribute. You won't get stressed with editing, creating the cover and other tasks included in writing a book. Moreover, you can use your CreateSpace copy as your submission to Kirkus.

Marketing your eBook is a big part of what will make your sales. It does not only involve advertising. It also involves looking for the right market and the means of getting your eBook out there. Though marketing has a lot of concepts surrounding it, everything mentioned in this chapter will equip you with all the information you need to make continuous money from your eBook.

Chapter 8 – Making Real Money

You are through with most of the hard work and it's time to make some cash out of all your effort. This chapter will discuss the many ways on how you can sell your eBook and many other ways on how you can make profit from it. Truth be told, there are dozens of ways you can keep the money coming in and it all depends on your willingness to try out these approaches.

Sell Through Multiple Retailers

This is the best way you can make money directly from your eBook. The million dollar question is how you can sell it. Let's take a look at one of the most famous landscapes in the eBook industry:

Kindle

At present, there are more than 400,000 titles in Kindle in the UK alone. Kindle allows you to self-publish your book. However, to make a reasonable profit, your eBook needs to be at least on the first 3% of highest ranking books. This is challenge but it can be done. It all lies on how you create marketing efforts. Another tip would be to price your eBook appropriately. If you have a very lengthy book, it would be smarter to split in into parts so you can sell it for a cheaper price. If the reader enjoys it, then they would buy the next one again. This is a strategy that many self-publishers practice. Once your book is out on Kindle, get the word out there through your website or through social media websites. The most valuable tip I could give you is to stick with KDP (Kindle Direct Publishing) https://kdp.amazon.com/. I recommend you do not experiment with other eBook platforms until you perfect this method of self-publishing as you may end up spending too much for registration fees until you are profitable. The standard conversion tool is a simple ".doc" MS Word file that Amazon converts to the Kindle format.

If you are not comfortable with Kindle, you can use other eBook stores you can check out online. There are lots of eBook stores out there such as Barnes & Nobles, BooksOnboard, eHarlequin eBook store and many more. Basically, the rules are quite the same but the prices may vary. You mainly give them a copy of your book, price it and then sell it through their platform. The differences may lie on the compatibility of your eBook with devices. For example, Amazon eBooks works with Kindle Reader and Barnes & Noble eBooks work with Nook Reader. Below are a few links to these eBook publishers:

List of Popular eBook Publishers

This is a list of popular eBook publishers and new author favorites. It is by no means a complete list but will get you started in publishing:

Payhip

Payhip will help you do most of the hard work: host your eBooks and securely deliver the eBooks to your customers. It will also handle payments through PayPal for you; all you have to do is upload your eBook to start selling. Once your eBook is on the site, you can promote your book anywhere (FaceBook, Twitter) with a link for your eBook page.

Royalty: 100%

Lulu

Lulu has a wide network of retail partners through which your eBook can reach readers, including the iBookstore and Barnes & Noble NOOK. You are even given the flexibility to set your own price. You can begin your eBook journey with their free eBook Creator Guide.

Royalty: 90%

Amazon Kindle Direct Publishing

If you know eBooks, you should also know what the Kindle eReader is. Publishing here would mean your books are on the Amazon Kindle Store and at the fingertips of many eBook users. Get started here or watch a <u>video tutorial</u> on how to publish eBooks on Kindle Direct Publishing.

Royalty: 35% to 70%

Smashwords

Publishing your eBook on Smashwords means it'll be able to reach the Apple iBookstore, Barnes & Noble, Sony Reader Store, Kobo, the Diesel eBook Store, Baker & Taylor's Blio and Axis360 and more. By registering, you're entitled to free ISBNs and eBook conversion to 9 formats. Here is a comprehensive guide: <u>Self-Publish an EBook with Smashwords</u>.

Royalty: 60% to 85%

Kobo Writing Life

With Kobo Writing Life you can reach out to millions of readers in over 170 countries. It is a do-it-yourself eBook publishing portal which makes your book available within their main catalogue, on any device. Just start out by bringing your own written materials to them in a simple Word document format and they'll convert it into a complete eBook for you.

Royalty: 70% - 80%

PubIt!

PubIt!, powered by Barnes & Noble, is where you can self-publish your books, ideas and content easily. It has a free conversion service to turn your work to be compatible with the NOOK, and other mobile or computing devices. You are however to pay them a slight cut off your royalty per sale since you're able to reach a high number of readers through Barnes & Noble.

Royalty: 40% - 65%

Booktango

Booktango is a free service that helps you design a cover for your eBook and then helps you publish and market it. You can sell your eBook through their connection of major retailers which includes Barnes & Noble, Apple iBookstore, Kobo, Sony, Amazon, Google and Scribd.

Royalty: 100%

MyeBook

MyeBook is a free web service that allows you to create, publish and get your inspirational content for the world to read. If you have a few eBooks that you want to sell, you can promote your 'bookstore' through a link (myeBook.com/my/*username*). With PayPal integration, your payments will also be smooth and hassle free.

Royalty: 90%

Blurb

Blurb has an online eBook creator to get you started. Edit and design your eBook on a simulated Apple iPad display. Once you've finished editing the content and design, your eBook will be ready to be sold on Blurb or the Apple iBookstore.

Royalty: 80%

E-Junkie

E-Junkie offers a simpler alternative to selling eBooks – sell them in PDF format. They also offer eBook security through 'PDF Stamping' where the buyers name, email address and transaction ID will be 'stamped' on the top right corner of each page to discourage unauthorized sharing your materials.

Royalty: 100%

Scribd

Scribd can help you manage and promote your work, while keeping track of your sales and earnings. However, to be able to sell on the Scribd Store, you'll require a seller account which is only available for users in the United States, Canada, Australia and United Kingdom.

Royalty: 80%

eBookMall

If you already have your eBook ready, you can list them at eBookMall and earn a percentage off every sale. eBookMall accepts both PDF and ePub formats. However, bear in mind that if you submit your eBooks to eBookMall directly through this program, your eBooks will not have DRM.

Royalty: 50%

eBookIt!

eBooktIt takes you through the steps of converting your writing into a professional eBook to be distributed through major eBook retailers which include Amazon, Apple, Barnes & Noble, Google, Sony, Ingram, and Kobo. You have to pay a fee for the processing and conversion of your writings into proper eBook formats, which cuts down the royalty that you can make from it.

Royalty: 50% - 80%

Tradebit

It doesn't matter if you see yourself as a poet or a technical writer – Tradebit enables you to publish your book/content/writings within a matter of seconds. You can start selling your file on eBay or on your homepage immediately. Download the Tradebit quick start tutorial here.

Royalty: 70% - 85%

ClickBank

ClickBank offers a unique online retail environment for digital products including eBooks. With a one-time product activation fee of $49.95, you are ready to promote your writings to more than 100,000 of ClickBank's active affiliate marketers.

Royalty: 50% - 90%

PaySpree

List your eBooks in PaySpree marketplace for instant exposure to thousands of potential new customers and affiliates. As a vendor you are allowed to list one product for free. If you want to add more products there is a one-time Premier account ($29 to activate) which entitles you to list an unlimited number of products for life.

Royalty: 90% - 100%

Click2Sell

You'll be able to publish and sell eBooks online without any startup costs. Click2Sell will store your eBook on secure servers and deliver it instantly to buyers after successful payment – everything will be done automatically for you. You will receive protection against illegal file sharing by customers as Click2Sell encrypts and protects it.

Royalty: 90% - 95%

Instabuck

With Instabuck you can sell digital products which also includes eBooks. With a premium account you'll get more features like product development and customer support handled for you. There is also an iOS app that you can use to keep track of your sales. With support of PayPay, ClickBank and AlertPay, money is instantly paid to you.

List of alternative eBook Publishers

Here is a list of useful eBook publishers; however each may have different requirements for your submission. Also, if you diversify publishers, you might not be able to take full advantage of some of the marketing tools Amazon has to offer, such as the Kindle Lending Library, where you can earn money just from someone borrowing your book from their library as a Prime customer.

Atlantic Bridge http://www.atlanticbridge.net/

Author House http://www.authorhouse.com/

Awe-Struck E-Books http://www.awe-struck.net/

Belgrave House http://www.belgravehouse.com/

Cobblestone Press http://www.cobblestone-press.com/

Creative Guy Publishing http://www.creativeguypublishing.com/

Diskus Publishing http://www.diskuspublishing.com/

Dorling Kindersley http://www.dk.com/

Double Dragon Publishing http://www.double-dragon-ebooks.com/

Draumr Publishing http://www.draumrpublishing.com/

eBook Publishing.us http://www.ebookpublishing.us/

ebooksonthenet.net http://www.ebooksonthe.net/

Echelon Press Publishing

http://www.echelonpress.com/

Electron Press http://www.electronpress.com/

Ellora's Cave Romantica

http://www.ellorascave.com/

Fiction-Net http://www.fiction-net.com/

Freya's Bower http://www.freyasbower.com/

GWP http://www.gate-way-publishers.com/

Hard Shell Word Factory

http://www.hardshell.com/

Highland Press http://www.highlandpress.org/

Loose Id, LLC http://www.loose-id.com/

Mojo Castle Press http://www.mojocastle.com/

Moxie Press http://www.moxiepress.com/

New Romance Books

http://www.blackvelvetseductions.com/

Pulpless.com http://www.pulpless.com/

Romance at Heart Publications

http://rahpubs.com/

Salvo Press http://www.salvopress.com/

Samhain Publishing

http://www.samhainpublishing.com/

Scorpius Digital Publishing

http://www.scorpiusdigital.com/

SynergEbooks http://www.synergebooks.com/

Torquere Press http://www.torquerepress.com/

Twilight Times Books

http://www.twilighttimesbooks.com/

Uncial Press http://www.uncialpress.com/

Zeus Publications http://www.zeus-publications.com/

The Importance of Book Reviews

When people buy your books, encourage them to submit their reviews. Reviews are very important because it can influence future buyers to make a purchase. This is another reason why you need to perfect your book before publishing it – you don't want negative reviews. 1 bad review can trump over 10 good reviews. Amazon has a very peculiar search engine spider that is based on the number of reviews one has. The more reviews, the better as you get ranked well above other authors with fewer or no reviews. NO REVIEWS = NO SALES!

Multiple Streams of Income

Obviously, the very first way for you to be able to sell eBooks is by selling them through the platforms discussed above. But, besides that, is there any other ways on how you can generate income from what you have written?

Yes. There are multiple ways on how you can make the income rolling in through your eBook.

Create a Website or Blog with Your Niche

Once you get your eBook out there, you must immediately make a website or a blog that your readers and future fans can follow for the many more books you will publish. For example, if your eBook is about aromatherapy, create a blog with the same niche and post articles regarding the topic as well. Once your website goes viral, you can already make money from selling stuff, books and through Google AdSense. The key here is in creating content with the right keywords as mentioned in our previous chapters. These keywords are the top most searched by users of the internet. This trick is called Search Engine Optimization and aids in making your website land at the top page of search engines. The higher your rank is, the more visitors or website hits you get and the more income you generate.

Open an Online Store

Consider your website as well as your online store. You won't need eBay and Amazon most especially if your website ranks high already. So, since your niche is on aromatherapy, you will be able to sell essential oils and other related items through that website. In no time, you will notice that you are making as much money from selling eBooks and selling your products.

Become an Affiliate

Affiliate marketing is basically a type of program where a business owner rewards an affiliate for every sale made. Thus, from this definition, you will need to welcome other authors or entrepreneurs in your circle. For example, you can place a page in your website entitled "Related Books" or "Suggested Books". Basically, these books are those you suggest your readers to take a look at. Meaning if they loved your own eBook then they will enjoy these books as well. Just be careful not to choose eBooks that are potential competition. Just choose those who are related to your niche.

When you choose to be an affiliate, you will get a commission from selling a copy of the book of another author. 10% would be a reasonable commission but of course, there could be other terms that a merchant (the retailer or the brand, in this case the other author) would have in mind. Just make sure the offer is reasonable and that you would make a commission that's acceptable to you.

The most important concept to remember in eBook publishing is marketing and reviews, even above the content itself. It is customer sales that drive your profitability and you need to get your book out in front of as many people as possible. Sometimes that may mean giving it away for free or lowering the price significantly.

Conclusion

Congratulations on taking the first step in your new writing and publishing endeavor by buying and reading this book! If you think this valuable information is useful and you feel inspired, please leave an Amazon review for this eBook. If you e-mail me at gerry.marrs@gmail.com I will also return the favor and review and provide a comment for your new eBook or send you a free Kindle ebook.

Let me know your success story and I'll also include you in my next eBook as well.

If you use the information in this eBook there is no reason at all you can't make a fulltime income (at least $2,000 per month every month consecutively based on average Kindle sales) by writing and publishing your own Kindle books. The market is literally exploding with new authors every day, and getting your new book ranked in the top 100 is not an impossible task. As a matter of fact, Amazon Kindle Direct Publishing offers services to help you easily market your book such as engaging in limited time free offers. This stimulates interest in your book and also raises it to the top of the best seller Top 100 list. Authors do this also with the hopes of generating positive review comments and star rankings. The magic number in reviews seems to be 6. With 6 reviews your book is prioritized by Amazon's rank listing over all others with fewer reviews. You'll be on top in no time at all generating sales. It is so exciting to open up a KDP report and see the number of sales instantly increase without having to lift a finger.

Price seems to be another sales generator. Some experts agree that .99 seems to be the new magic price to generate sales but others feel that such a low price devalues their work and takes away from potentially large profits. It's certainly a valid consideration considering the amount of time and effort; however, in brick and mortar publishing houses, the residual royalties are actually much lower; more like .17 per book. So if you take that into consideration, a lower Kindle price on your book is still a better deal. Many Kindle millionaires have been made using the .99 cent price option.

Your new eBook does not have to be 150 pages to be successful. Most new top-selling eBooks are under 50 pages, with just the right amount of information customer are seeking. With many having busy schedules and busy lives, it's difficult to get your point across if you include extraneous filler just to increase the volume size of your book. It's no longer necessary and your customers will appreciate you being direct and to the point.

Another extremely exciting aspect of publishing eBooks is worldwide recognition. Depending upon the publisher you use, your book will be available to a global audience. Using your eBook publishing website, you can download a customizable report that shows individual sales from other countries (Kindle specifically has this using a drop-down menu to show which Amazon sites a download or purchase occurred from).

As you can see, writing and publishing eBooks is more than just making money. It's an exciting opportunity to reach out and touch thousands of lives through your words.

I hope you get inspired to do great things!

Gerry Marrs

Gerry.marrs@gmail.com

Twitter: https://twitter.com/GerryMarrs

About the Author

Gerry Marrs is a research specialist who enjoys helping people and giving back to his community. He started a homeless meals program in his neighborhood which is now on complete auto-pilot, serving free meals to over 400 local homeless vets and those who struggle with addictions each month. He enjoys writing in his spare time on a variety of topics and hopes to build a successful portfolio of "how to" products designed to help people struggling with a variety of issues.

He is currently working on a Ph.D. in Business Administration and while not immersed in dissertation writing, is raising two successful kids, and loves Disney World. He currently lives on the Gulf Coast in Florida along the world's most beautiful beaches.

Other Books by Gerry Marrs available through Amazon

How to Legally Rob Credit-Card Companies: Get Out of Debt Faster, Raise Your Credit Score, and Finally Live Free!

How to Burn Fat and Lose Weight Ridiculously Easy: Even During the Holidays

How to Write, Edit, and Self-Publish Your First eBook: Make Money Writing Instant International Bestsellers!

How to Make $800 Per Month: Starting Tonight! A "no-hype" realistic plan you can implement immediately, without spending a dime of your own!

The Beach Body Way to a Healthier Lifestyle: Improve Your Diet, Reduce Stress, and Enjoy Amazing Sex